C000163366

1

First Published in 2020
001
Requests for permission to reproduce material from this work should be sent to the
Author directly at:

15 Stratton Street
London
W1J 8LQ

Jacket Art: Author's own work. "Wheat Fields", Dhruv Sharma.

Copyright © Dhruv Sharma, 2020

The moral right of the author has been asserted. In addition, Dhruv Sharma has asserted his right under the Copyright, Designs and Patents Act, 1988, to be identified as Author of this work.

A CIP Catalogue record for this book is available from the British Library.

Library of Congress Cataloging-in-Publication-Data

Names: Sharma, Dhruv, author.
Title: Financial History of Asian Private Equity, 1990-2020
Identifiers: LCCN 2020918817

Type Set in 7, 8, 9, 10, 12, and 24pt Georgia

ISBN: 979-8687923385

10 9 8 7 6 5 4 3 2 1

Financial History of Asian Private Equity, 1990-2020

"Recognize that ultimate success comes from opportunistic, bold moves which, by definition, cannot be planned."

Bryan Burrough, Barbarians at the Gate

Contents

Introduction

As Heterogeneous as the Asian Landmass is, there are linkages and common features shared across Private Equity Development since the late-20th Century across its many continental divides; however within a single lifetime, Private Equity has become an intrinsic form and pillar to Asian Economic Development and has contributed to the re-rise of Asia towards its return as the centre of world trade and economic activity into the mid-21st Century. In part it is led by the Asian Tigers as well as sectoral opening in behemoth states of India and China; previously state owned becoming private businesses to be openly controlled and sold. Legal frameworks for arbitration and corporate governance have significantly improved and protected private equity investors from malfeasance, as well as giving minority rights to growth investors who previously would have been sidelined. Conversely, in humanity's biggest expansion of growth and prosperity, Asian private equity is an expression of ruthless capitalism which at times without a public form of disclosure and governance has given expression to fraud and outright rampant growth at the expense of labour and social goods.

The structure of this book is to take each major Asian geographic region separately and then to draw conclusions at the very end on the success and viability of Private Equity Investing through Asia as well as providing a note on its future path into the 2020s and 2030s. Due to its increasingly Asian Links and Trade Flows, Australian Private Equity is given a chapter in this book as well and treated to be intrinsically part of the same Asian narrative. The book draws upon the Author's Investing Experience across Asia as well as discussions had with public policymakers and local investors and private equity firms, the author has met, partnered up with, and carried Due Diligence upon; without delving too deeply into the Author's biases, the book takes an overarching narrative and descriptive form to provide an overview on the development and structural evolution of Private Equity across Asia with further footnoted references provided therein.

I define Private Equity covering all forms of sector ownership, ranging from Consumer Technology to Retail to Energy Service Providers; Investors buying these businesses range from private equity fund managers, who in turn have their own investors investing onto their General Partner-Limited Partner ('GP-LP') structures which vary in shape, size, term, and form, to other family businesses and strategic and corporate investors. The usual PE investment is characterized by an indirect model whereby investors invest via an intermediary, the General Partner ("GP"). These funds are raised from other investors (the "LPs") and then invested for usually over a decade and are governed by subscription and partnership agreements between the LPs and the principal partners in the fund which specifies the nature of the fund's activities and the division of the proceeds and profits therein to the LP and GP. Unlike other asset management industries, such as Hedge Funds for which the US and UK share almost 90% of the global market by firm location, Private Equity is fundamentally a local industry and requires cultural nous, self-awareness, and certain depth of knowledge across fields.

Professional Asian Private Equity Investors, namely managers and firms managing third party capital on commercial terms, manage a smaller portion of GDP and Public Market Capitalisation compared to the similar for European and U.S. Economies. In India, Private Equity ("PE") AUM managed internally as of 2019 is $28 Billion, exactly the same AUM for South East Asia, and there is more than $50 Billion in Korea. Outside of China, this steady AUM growth of PE has been reflective of more of a natural, than state led or deterministic, progression of the development of Asian Private Equity; which is in stark contrast to the state owned enterprises who have commanded and steered production from Japan to China in the 20th Century. Across Asia-Pacific, Professional Private Equity AUM has peaked to around $900 Billion leading upto 2020, more than a quarter of global AUM within the asset class. Serving as a conduit for the world's savings as it becomes PE's largest market for investment, demand, and growth into the mid-21st century. AUM in Asian Private Equity will continue to grow as intermediation and principal-agent relationships are key to be able to invest prudently across and within Asia and tap its growth potential this century from it burgeoning middle classes whilst adhering to unwritten local social and legal customs as well as red tape which is so prevalent even in the more developed Asian economies.

Structurally, Asian Private Equity Funds have become more investor friendly in particular when adopting European Waterfall on Carry Distributions as opposed to the American Waterfall, which provides a carry distribution schedule on a deal by deal basis and can often, due to boom-bust economic cycle overlaps with the fund life, lead to clawbacks wherein too much carry has been paid at the initial stages of the fund compared to later stages. European waterfall is fairer and relies on an aggregate fund level distribution.[1]

---

[1] The foremost compilation of respective registered managers active in Asian Private Equity and Venture are compiled by the respective country associations and regulatory authorities detailing also their respective regulations, structures, and performances:

Australia
https://www.avcal.com.au/
https://asic.gov.au/
India
https://ivca.in/
https://www.sebi.gov.in/
Korea
http://www.kvca.or.kr/en/
http://meng.fsc.go.kr/
China
http://www.cvca.org.cn/aboutcvca/profile.asp
http://www.cbrc.gov.cn/showyjhjjindex.do
Japan
http://www.japanpea.jp/english/about/index.html

Private equity has grown sharply in Asia-Pacific in the decade upto 2020 with almost $883bn under management which represent 26 percent of the global private equity market in 2018. In 2008, the similar share was 17 percent. Within the region, private equity investments have become more balanced geographically. Despite the greater role of China, which takes 45 percent of private equity activity, India and Japan each represented more than 10 percent of total deal value. By 2017, the number of Asia-Pacific funds amounted to 194, with average sizes of $340mn, while in the period 2012–2016 the average number of funds were 325, with average size of $190mn. PE Deal multiples have also gone up, as expressed against the EBITDA of target companies, from 3-4x in the 2000s to upto 8-10x in 2010s peaking at a median deal multiple of 14x by 2018.[2] Performance also varies greatly amongst GPs by as much as 15% IRR between the bottom and top quartiles and much of the difference is accounted by managerial inexperience in Asian markets when controlling for fund size, country focus, and first time strategies.

Fundamentally Private Equity is a structural form to allow investors across borders to invest into businesses which are commercially

---

https://jvca.jp/en/members/vc-members
https://www.fsa.go.jp/en/
Singapore (South East Asia)
https://www.svca.org.sg/
https://www.mas.gov.sg/

[2] "Is Asian private equity still an attractive play?" Business Times Singapore, 29th May 2019.

viable. Private Equity provides for a structure which catalyzes this Foreign Direct Investment and protects the principal's capital through universal norms of governance, control, and fee economics. That's why it works and continues to provide gains both for the principal, the LP, and the agent, the GP. Subtleties exist in Asian Private Equity where many an Asian Corporate, especially across East Asia, are averse to fund management and thus tend to establish crossborder corporate venturing and private equity type permanent vehicles set up to diversify and provide portfolio strategic gains to the parent corporate.

Asian Private equity still lags behind its western counterparts on distributions and realised exits. There is still the abstract promise of Asian Private Equity than its actual success. Another aspect hampering growth is the lack of larger funds to accommodate increasing ticket commitments from US and Sovereign Investors; many of whom are used to making at least $100mn single commitments into any given fund. The catch-22 here is that for sector focussed strategies and country specific funds in Asia, often a fund larger than $500mn is hard to invest in any given economic cycle without trampling over fund risk and strategy parameters.

Furthermore, Asian Funds, especially growth focussed, do not have the deal flow run rate nor the investors domestically to raise their fund sizes to accommodate these capital patterns within Private Equity in the past decade. Fundamentally, the cyclically adjusted risk reward mix is also on thin grounds for Asian private equity, at least comparable to Europe and US Buyout Strategies where 2-3x gross multiple on invested capital over any given decade is a reasonable reward for the illiquidity premium and counterparty risks undertaken there. In Asia, a commensurate analysis, ceteris paribus, would demand at least a 5-6x multiple over any given decadal economic cycle and counterparty risks; in addition to counterparty risks, mismatched economics cycles, significant trade and exit barriers, and other exogenous factors are all too common across Asia since World War II. During the beginning of the period of this book, following the 1997 Asian Financial Crisis, a cross-comparison of returns between US and Asian Private Equity was grossly stark; between 1997 and 2001, US PE recorded an IRR of 16.6% against a negative 3.3% returns from Asia over the same period.[3] In many ways it reflected more the unsophisticated manner of Private Equity Investing in an Asian Wild West than the Financial Crisis impacts of that time. Many GPs in Asia in the 1990s would mostly make punts into pre-IPO Minority positions than do growth or buyout investing.

In the 2020 Pandemic Crisis, Global Private Equity will be reacting in two folds. Firstly, private equity GPs who did not buy enough in the depths of the global financial crisis of 2008 will be more active in buying good underlying businesses, sometimes at deep cyclical discounts. Secondly, the private equity model in 2020 is a different beast to the 2008 model. There is more global dry powder, an estimated $1.4 trillion, much of it held by largecap Buyout Funds situated in the US and UK; Private Equity GPs have the experience of

---

[3] "Has Asia's safe haven been oversold?", Euromoney, September 2002.

the 2008 GFC to draw on as well as having more widespread operational experience in-house; to its advantage for flexibility, private equity now has far deeper and more flexible global secondaries markets, and greater access to data from a wider range of comparable and sector focussed portfolio companies whose business models are replicable across borders. These attributes suggest that private equity will prove its worth to institutional portfolios during the early 2020s, as it did during the 2008-2012 period and recovery. 2020 then also provides a neat demarcation to understand and study Private Equity's evolution upto 2020 from the early 1990s when much of Asia was still emerging.

Any errors are mine alone and I would like to thank the Clients of Marcena Capital Ltd and colleagues in providing ongoing professional support in helping me to build and often correct my understanding of the nuances in play across Asian private markets. As a global citizen over the last decade upto 2020, I have spent increasingly more time in empathising, meeting, and acknowledging the potential to change lives across this magnificently diverse and rich supercontinent from Baotou, Inner Mongolia, to Hobart, Tasmania!

Dhruv Sharma

London, England
September 2020

China

China

**Selected
Private Market
Funds**

1990	
	1993- Infinity Nitzanim Fund $27mn
	1998- Infinity I Fund $91mn
	1999- Carlyle Asia Partners $750mn
2000	2001-Hony Capital Fund I $38mn
	2001- Infinity II Fund $64mn
	2001- Legend Capital Fund I $35mn
	2004-Hony Capital Fund II $88mn
	2005- CITIC Equity Partners $45mn
	2006-CITIC Equity Partners II $61mn
	2006- Infinity Israel-China Fund $263mn
	2006- Sequoia Capital China I $260mn
	2008-Hony Capital RMB Fund I RMB 5.2Bn
	2008- Legend Capital Fund IV $350mn
	2010-Carlyle Asia Partners III $2.8bn
	2010- Sequoia Capital China III $1Bn
2010	2011- Hony Capital RMB Fund II RMB 10Bn
	2011- Primavera Capital Fund I $1bn
	2011- CITIC Capital International Partners III $562mn
	2013- Goodman Hong Kong Fund $300mn
	2014- Carlyle Asia Partners IV $3.9Bn
	2014- HighLight Capital Fund I $190mn
	2016- Hony Capital Fund VIII $2.7bn
	2016-Warburg Pincus China Fund I $2bn
	2016- Primavera Capital Fund II $1.9Bn
	2017- DCP Capital Fund $2bn
	2019-Primavera Capital Fund III $3.4bn
	2019-Warburg Pincus China-SEA II $4.25bn
2020	2019- CITIC Capital China Partners IV $2.8bn
	2019- Sequoia Capital China Growth Fund V $1.8Bn

China encompasses almost 40% of the roughly $600Bn raised since 2008 in Asia-Pacific Private Equity Funds and by 2019 it has become the third largest private equity and venture market globally deploying almost $66bn.[4] A division between old and new economy sectors are reflecting the relative successes of Chinese private equity vintages. New economy sectors include advanced manufacturing, e-commerce, and healthcare whereas old economy sectors include industrials, automotive, and property. These new economy sectors constitute 85% of the growth in Chinese Private Equity Valuations and 80% of the total fund strategies. Increasing competition for these new economy sectors are reflected in the entry multiple disparity existing with the old economy; 26x entry multiple on enterprise to EBITDA on new versus 13x for old. Taking into account this background, the allocation strategies of foreign LPs towards China PE has increasingly moved towards gaining access through indigenous GPs over

---

[4] "In search of alpha: Updating the playbook for private equity in China", McKinsey & Company, 27th August 2020.

pan-Asian or US-based GPs, the former providing competitive market access, proprietary deal flow, and cultural self-awareness as a second generation of professional domestic GPs forms in China going into 2020. DCP Capital, coming out of KKR in 2017, and Centurium Capital, formed by former-Warburg Pincus Head of Asia Pacific, have been the latest evolution of local spin outs from western blue chip GPs which began with Capital Today in 2005, founded by Kathy Xu former Baring PE Head of China. The trend towards buyout investing is also becoming more prominent over growth strategies through the course of the 2010s.

Although China's economic development has closely tracked the state-driven models, first led by Japan and Asian Tigers in the latter half of the 20th Century, its cheap credit and overinvestment into superfluous and underused infrastructure and private investment into speculative property has created a deep cyclical debt burden from the early 1990s to 2020. China's Private Equity industry was established in the mid-1980s, when the Chinese state decided that it should develop indigenous high-tech services oriented industries, leaving the manufacturing base in the hands of archaic state backed entities. The first fund was established in 1985 by the central government when the State Science and Technology Commission and the Ministry of Finance joined together to create China New Technology Venture Investment Corporation. Local governments followed suit and established their own regional funds acting more as regional sovereign development funds and acting as conduits for cheap equity into the local industrial base than growth private equity.

Many of these early private equity participants in China lacked expertise, basic governance models, and external market supporting institutions which would otherwise provide defined property rights, freedom of contract, and financial markets. All these did not exist in the late 1980s and early 1990s in post-Maoist China.

As economic and financial reforms began to open China to foreign direct investment, the central government began to officially encourage foreign GPs to invest in China in 1995 which triggered the first wave of PE Flows, mostly from the US. China's private equity industry expanded gradually from the early 2000s on the country's accession to the WTO, at least compared to the rapid progress being made in the US and Europe and even other parts of Asia such as Australia. Nevertheless, a number of largecap deals were encouraged and Foreign GPs like Carlyle bought into China Pacific Life, paying $408mn for a 25% stake in 2005, and TPG reportedly making almost a 16x return on its 2004 investment into Shenzhen Development Bank.[5]

By the late 2000s, a growing distinction was forming in the Chinese PE industry between GPs that styled themselves on the governance of a foreign GP and funds that looked a lot like a government operation. Amongst the former, CITIC started closing a series of ever larger RMB funds and, amongst the latter, powerfully well connected domestic GPs launched industrial investment funds, including

---

[5] "Foreign private equity funds aim to act local in China", Global Capital Asiamoney, September 2010.

Tianjin government's Bohai Industrial Investment Fund in 2007. Upto 2009, Foreign GPs were not allowed to set up RMB Funds and had to rely on a 'Sina Model' to allow for offshore control rights and profits routed from China-based entities which themselves were upheld by a complicated array of contracts with their offshore SPVs.[6]

Government policy change in 2005 resulted in the further gradual revival of domestic GPs through the opening of the Small and Medium Enterprise Board, which provided an exit mechanism for domestic GPs; much of the impetus coming from the raft of exits of PE-backed Chinese Companies on the US Exchanges, notably Linktone, SMIC, Shanda, and KongZhong in 2004. Although only a very few RMB domestic GPs were able to access foreign exchanges for IPOs. In addition, the number of renminbi denominated funds grew after amendments to the Partnership Enterprise Law in 2006 allowing the use of limited partnerships for domestic Chinese LPs to invest into their own local onshore funds; this too because some of the successful exits made up to then were backed by Foreign GP and Corporate Strategics, Motorola and Temasek in SMIC, Softbank's SB Asia Infrastructure Fund behind Shanda, and DFJ in KongZhong.

Overall these reforms did not dampen the enthusiasm for US exits for Chinese Investments, by 2010 almost 125 mainland Chinese companies were listed on the NASDAQ.[7] Some Foreign GPs did list on the local and Hong Kong Markets, notably KKR made 3.3x on their

[6] China as an Innovation Nation, Zhou, Lazonick, and Sun, 2019.
[7] "Private Equity, All Aboard?", Newstex Web Blogs, 19th October 2010.

$150mn investment into China Modern Dairy upon its HK Listing in 2010.

By 2010, a number of foreign GP and state-led domestic partnerships flourished including Blackstone's partnership with the Government of Shanghai to launch the Blackstone Zhonghua Development Investment Fund focussed on Shanghai in 2009; Carlyle launching a RMB Fund with the backing of Beijing's municipal government in 2010; 80% owned by Carlyle with Beijing's BSCOMC taking 20% interest; and TPG forming a similar partnership with the Chongqing government in the TPG Western China Growth Partners I. Most of these partnerships from the perspective of Chinese local governments was to build the ecosystem of their then emerging financial centres by bringing in these marquee Global GP names. Overall, the number of total dealmaking reached a combined $230bn between 2001 and 2012 but exits were much rarer, relying almost entirely on IPOs creating by 2013 a backlog of almost 900 companies wanted to list on the Shanghai and Shenzhen markets and aggravated by a spate of listed Chinese scandals on the US Exchanges.[8]

By the onset of the GFC in 2008, a group of nascent emerging domestic GPs identified by Foreign LPs as credible and trustworthy led to a notable concentration in GPs who were able to obtain USD Funds from Foreign LPs. Notably, FountainVest was able to secure $200mn apiece from two of Canada's most active PE LPs, CPPIB and

---

[8] "Private Equity in China: Which Way Out?", New York Times, 10th January 2013.

Teaches' Private Capital, in 2008. Motorola, who had almost $3.6bn investments by 2005 in China alone in electronics, sought to become an LP in a number of Chinese Venture USD Funds, including participating in a $35mn fund in 2006 of Shanghai NewMargin Venture. Domestic venture GPs affiliated to investment banks and securities firms also experienced rapid growth after 2007 as they were previously prohibited from making equity investments in their pre-IPO clients. This trend became so successful that by 2020, Investment Banks, like China Renaissance, established co-investing funds, both in USD and RMB, cherry picking deals being advised on by their investment banking unit. Even during the 2020 Pandemic they raised a growth fund which now had begun to lead on deals, Huaxing Growth Capital Fund III in USD.

In 2009 the Growth Enterprise Board acted as a venture board and which introduced a new exit venue for VC investments. Further, the introduction of the New Third Board in 2012 offered small businesses a financing alternative and has created more dynamic and diverse capital markets. In addition, fundraising for domestic GPs benefited from the increased assets of state controlled institutions such as pension funds and local insurers. Chinese insurance companies have been allowed to invest up to 10% of their total assets in both domestic and offshore funds since 2010. By 2015, many local insurers began to compete with domestic GPs by establishing their own internal PE Funds leading to almost 19 of these funds being created by 2019 worth RMB130Bn.[9] Over the late 2010s, the central government, alongside its banking and financial regulators, have encouraged local insurers to take on the role traditionally provided by Banks to become more active in PE and also to discourage the 'cash pooling' activities of the latter.

Despite these institutional reforms since the 1980s, Distributions remain low even for 2007-11 PE fund vintages at 0.8x and 2011-14 vintages at 0.2x mostly due to them being growth minority strategies where exit situations are harder to control; venture returns were also suboptimal being around 2x for 2001-2005 vintages. More pertinently, the inexperience of the first generation of Chinese GPs showed especially those who were too persuaded by the PE model to make deals than actively manage portfolios which led to GP management turnover, lack of institutional experience, and often more sinister acts of fraud and failed corporate governance oversight.

Domestic investors tend to be China's National Pension Fund, Provincial Governments, State-owned Enterprises, and Insurers who are also increasingly risk averse and unsophisticated in their private equity selection in comparison to foreign LPs. Creating a self-selective situation by the mid-2010s where the best-in-class domestic GPs from China tend to raise both onshore RMB and offshore USD generation series funds. Both differ in their terms, expectations, and often strategies to cater to the professional scale of their disparate LP

---

[9] "Insurers gain a craving for China private equity", AsianInvestor, 30th June 2019.

bases. Limitations on strategy are also there due to increasing competition, even lower down the market, from State owned buyers, first wave of successful Chinese entrepreneurs born in the 1960s reluctant to relinquish family control over their businesses, as well as deep pocketed corporate new economy buyers.

Disparity exists also on the structure of USD and RMB Generation Funds, Foreign LPs seek to invest in funds that have five-year investment periods, 10-year terms, and which target multiples of 2-3x on their invested capital. Conversely, Chinese domestic LPs seek investments with much shorter holding periods of around one to three years and significantly higher returns at at least 4x to invested capital. In addition RMB Funds tend to have a smaller fund size compared to their foreign counterparts and typically call capital from their investors much less frequently; often just two or three times per year. Capital Call Default rates tend also to be higher with domestic LPs as well as fundraising periods between successive RMB Generation funds shorter for the GPs, often around a year between any two RMB Fund Generations.

Additionally, Foreign and domestic LPs differ in terms of the level of reporting and portfolio monitoring they expect from their GPs. Whilst offshore LPs are content with receiving quarterly reports, Chinese domestic LPs require more guidance, hand-holding through regular and elongated one-on-one meetings, to receive an update or discuss trivial portfolio developments. Chinese domestic LPs also often seek to involve themselves in the decision making of a GP; sometimes such control and influence is exercised often in the background without explicit disclosure to other investors.[10]

Nevertheless RMB funds have the simplest and fastest government approval process and are not faced with currency conversion issues; they also have the ability to invest in both old and new economy sectors. Foreign invested RMB funds are denominated in RMB and receive their capital from either foreign investors or a combination of foreign and domestic investors. They may offer some advantages over foreign currency funds, including more expedient regulatory approvals and may be increasingly used by Chinese GPs.

In 2016, almost two-thirds of the $72bn raised by Chinese PE and VC GPs was held in RMB Funds.[11] This climaxed to $93bn by 2017 before plummeting to $13bn in 2018.[12] Much of this reflected, by the late 2010s, in the tightening of Bank Credit as well as many inexperienced RMB domestic GPs jumping on the fundraising bandwagon but then struggling to exit from their sky high entry valuations. A crackdown on these rogue domestic RMB GPs, some of whom sold their products through banking and P2P platforms, began leading to almost 163

---

[10] "The Private Equity Limited Partnership in China: A Critical Evaluation of Active Limited Partners.", Lin, Journal of Corporate Law Studies, Vol. 13, No. 1, pp. 185-217, April 2013.

[11] "What lies ahead for China private equity", Private Equity International, 19th October 2017.

[12] "China Private Equity hit by share downturn", Financial Times, 15th March 2019.

private fund entities 'losing contact' with the government industry body, AMAC, in 2017.[13]

In the early 2010s, a focus towards NPLs and Distressed Investing rose amongst some GPs, part of the wider global trend following the 2008 GFC; by 2012 a number of GPs including Clearwater Capital Partners, Mount Kellett Capital, Q Capital, began raising distressed focussed funds with a core allocation to China. Many were encouraged to do so as in the earlier phase of debt cleanup, local Asset Management Companies dominated the secondary credit markets; four AMCs were established by the central government to sell NPLs worth RMB 1.4Tn following the 1997 Asian Financial Crisis.

By the end of decade up to 2020, China was now producing more start-ups valued at at least US$1 billion at a faster pace than the United States. One of the drivers of this evolution has been the behavior of Chinese consumers toward new products and online services; as well as maturity in the venture ecosystem as China's Internet Giants began acquiring more businesses across sectors ranging from financial services, gaming, education, health care, and artificial intelligence. These giants themselves were part of the first wave of VC boom in China, including the first generation of 'big three portals', Sina, Sohu, and Netease, and the second generation of even more successful, Baidu, Alibaba, and Tencent.

---

[13] "China private equity funds suffer wave of closures", Financial Times, 5th August 2018.

As of 2018, the number of Internet users in China had surpassed US users in adopting new apps for online entertainment, payments, education, and travel services. The average deal size in new economy sector increased to $213mn in 2018 from $30mn in 2013, since the huge volume of private equity and venture capital flowing into China's new economy has oversaturated the smaller deals, prompting investors to seek larger investments further up the scale and competing with domestic strategics and state corporates. Similar to PE Models, a number of cross border venture partnerships were formed starting with Accel Partners and IDG Technology Venture in 2005.

Chinese Venture saw a spectacular growth, initially in 1995 only 10 venture GPs were active, this eventually increased to 500 by 2005 and more than 5000 by 2012. Almost $53bn was invested in China over 7900 deals between Asian Financial Crisis and 2016.[14]

Appelbaum et al. wrote in 2018 that the Chinese government is involved in "picking winners, prioritizing industries, and betting on manufacturing stars".[15] Thus, many New Economy firms require certifications from the government, which in turn grants them preferable policies and market access. Even granting certification and presuming market access, nothing was certain for Chinese GPs, for instance with venture investments in Chinese e-commerce, startups often lacked one of the three: transparent information flow enabling

---

[14] China as an Innovation Nation, Zhou, Lazonick, and Sun, 2019.
[15] Innovation in China: Challenging the Global Science and Technology System, Appelbaum, Cao, Han, Parker, and Simon, John Wiley & Sons, 2018.

trust between customers, payments, and delivery. It took Alibaba imitating Paypal to resolve payments alone, through the successful creation of Alipay. Some of these firms lack innovation and secular growth due to this system wide structural issue of readily available state support, cheap credit, and grants. Lately, Chinese venture investments have supported world leading businesses active in image recognition, AI, and deep-learning software. In part a reluctance by ByteDance, forced to sell TikTok's US Arm, during the 2020 Pandemic when it took the ire of the Trump Administration was its proprietary and addictive machine learning algorithm developed in China; ByteDance itself was backed by a US GP, KKR.

Some private equity managers were established as offshoots to state groups, one such was Hony Capital, Spun out of state-backed Legend Holdings in 2003, and shot to prominence through a series of restructurings of other state-owned groups. As Hony grew, so did its appetite for foreign cross-border investments based on a strategy that China's increasingly richer and mobile middle class would be ready-made consumers of western brands, replicable across borders; this strategy has proved misplaced and highlighted by their disastrous investment into UK based Pizza Express bought in 2014 for $1.54bn.

In venture too a number of foreign corporate strategics failed to understand Chinese customers, notably eBay lost out to Taobao and Google was defeated by Baidu. On top of this, regulator restrictions immediately popped up in the mid-2010s towards Chinese outbound PE investments; including failed bids by China Resources and Hua

Capital to buy a US Chip maker, Fairchild, and GO Scale Capital's $2.8bn bid on Philips Lumileds Division. But given the attractions of Chinese capital as well as its apparent allure in the 2010s, a number of cross border GP partnerships fell short of delivery including a notorious partnership between the Russian Sovereign Fund, RDIF, and a Chinese GP called Inventis in 2016.[16]

Like elsewhere, the 2020 Pandemic has reset overheated valuations in the new economy sectors and allowed for further changes in a positive direction for Chinese Private Equity. More so as these New Economy valuations have been determined in the two decades upto 2020 by their traditional exit routes through IPO. Venture rounds are unlikely to get smaller in absolute size, but raising capital will take longer, down rounds are becoming more likely following earlier frothy valuations, and GPs will be more discerning. Activity following the 2020 Pandemic Lockdown in China did pick up, including Yuanfudao, an education startup, raising $1bn at a $7.8bn valuation and a number of venture GPs, including HighLight Capital, Qiming, IDG Capital, and Bytedance Venture Fund, securing foreign and domestic LPs during the course of 2020.

Although the availability of foreign exit channels have been crucial in providing credibility for the two decades up to 2020 to Chinese PE and VC investing, the transformation of local exit venues, such as in Shenzhen, and maturity of the venture and buyout ecosystems in

---

[16] "Inventis: In search of China's 'largest' PE firm", Private Equity International, 8th October 2018.

China has placed it to overtake the US by the end of the 2020s as the largest global PE market. Much of investing successfully in China is a tried and tested approach with the gut of intuition attached to it; for instance Sequoia backed Meituan, having watched their founder Xing Wang with two prior startups. Meituan provided Sequoia with far greater returns than its investment in Google.[17]

---

[17] "Can KKR expand from buyouts to backing young tech in Asia?", Financial Times, 16th September 2020.

Japan

Japan

1990

Selected
Private Market
Funds

1996- Globis Incubation Fund JPY 540mn
1997- MVC Global Japan Fund I $17mn
1998- TMCAP 98 JPY3.8bn ($40mn)
1999-Unison Capital Partners I JPY38bn ($380mn)
2000 2000-TMCAP2000 JPY 22bn

2003-JAFCO Technology Partners I $100mn
2004-Unison Capital Partners II JPY140bn ($1.4bn)
2006-Globis Fund III JPY 16bn
2006-SBI BB Mobile Investment JPY 32bn ($279mn)
2007-Advantage Partners Fund IV JPY 216bn ($1.9bn)

2009-Unison Capital Partners III JPY 140bn ($1.5bn)
2010 2010- JAFCO Technology Partners IV $100mn

2011- DRC II JPY 15.7B
2012- Goodman Japan Core Fund $1bn

2016-Globis Fund V JPY 26bn
2016-TMCAP2016 JPY51.7bn
2017-NSSK Fund II $530mn
2018-Icon Venture Fund $375mn
2018- Marunouchi Global Fund II $831mn
2019- ESR Japan Logistics Fund III JPY70bn
2020

Japanese Corporate Culture has been notorious for decades for its cultural hurdles, varying from an insular corporate governance environment to a lack of shareholder pressure on the board of directors of businesses there. Leading many Japanese conglomerates to hold onto underperforming businesses and to shy away from anglo saxon business models, most eagerly represented by Private Equity in the two decades up to 2020. Many Japanese management structures favour inaction over disrupting the tightly knit working fabric in favour of outside shareholders.

In 1997, Advantage Partners raised its maiden MBI Fund I from ten Japanese institutional investors, including Marubeni which provided a large portion of the JPY3 billion and took some control rights. Despite being formed in 1992, it took Advantage five years to raise a fund as only a regulatory change in 1996 allowed for a holding structure to acquire majority stakes in a Japanese company; indeed, the first Japanese buyout was carried out in December 1998 of ICS

Kokusai Bunka Kyoiku Center.[18] For the second fund, MBI Fund II in 2000, Advantage took 20% of its target raise from foreign LPs. By Fund V, Advantage took 35% of fund share from Foreign LPs.

Foreign LPs gained familiarity with the Japanese PE Market as a number of high profile banking deals were carried out in the eight year period of 1998-2006 by Foreign GPs: by Cerberus of Aozora Bank, Loan Star of Tokyo Star, Ripplewood of Shinsei/LTCB. The last was said to achieve a 12x return on Ripplewood's investment by 2005 having paid a token 1bn Yen for LTCB's equity in 2000 and a further $1Bn for its recapitalisation.[19] David Rubinstein had reportedly described it as "possibly the most profitable private equity deal of all time".[20] A public outcry followed amongst the Japanese media that non capital gains taxes were paid on exit leading the government passing a "Shinsei Tax".

In addition, domestic Financial Institutions also jumped on board the burgeoning PE market, with Nomura Principal Finance, Daiwa Securities SMBC Principal Investments, and Nikko Principal Investments; some of these entities already have a prior knowledge of PE, having been a lead debt supplier to Western Buyout GPs in the 1980s and 1990s, in particular Fuji Bank now Mizuho, and some of these entities were also LPs to the first wave of US Buyout GPs.

---

[18]M&A Finance, Sasayama and Muraoka, 2006, pg. 38.
[19] "Turnaround of the Year: Shinsei Bank", Buyouts Insider, 14th February 2015.
[20] "Big in Japan", PEI Asia, March 2007.

In the early 2000s, Japanese PE was aided by legal changes including the commercial law revision in 2001 and 2002 and further reform of company law in 2006. Under the 2002 revisions, businesses were able to choose on the advice of board members, allow outside directors more influence, and allow for more efficient share exchanges further enhanced by the 2006 company reforms allowing for triangular mergers.

By 2006, the three leading Japanese indigenous and independent GPs included Advantage Partners, MKS Partners, and Unison Capital. Nevertheless public and corporate perception in Japan of private equity led even these three GPs to often look at the same deals despite the size of the Japanese Economy. Most infamously all three were active in consortium acquisition in 2006 of Kanebo, a Household products firm. Even in the mid 2000s local GPs struggled to compete against the well resourced cash rich domestic buyers attached to Japanese Financial Institutions. Nevertheless, due to the lack of competition in the small-cap space, many local GPs in the 2000s earned 10x multiples on these low hanging fruits; notably Advantage bought CommunityOne, a small property developer, in 2008 and exited it for 23x.[21]

Japanese Venture Capital has had a longer history stemming from the 1980s, when Schroder Ventures had a dedicated Japanese Venture Fund of $24mn, however back then much of this capital was targeting mature businesses pre-IPO with mezzanine equity; JAFCO was the

---

[21] "The Long Goodbye", Finance Asia, 26th September 2016.

most prominent, acting as a subsidiary of Nomura Securities. Even in the early 2000s, most self-declared venture GPs pursued buyouts of mature IT or consumer facing businesses; notably Phoenix Capital, brough Sakuraya, a mass retailer in the Tokyo Metro, for 4bn Yen in 2004.

By the mid-2000s, Corporate Venturing also lagged behind established US norms as many incubators formed in Tokyo sought for long term holds over short exit leading to a 'commons' type tragedy where the ecosystem fell short following Series A funding; in fact in 2008, almost a third of Japanese venture funding went to later stage startups with retail investor scepticism on premature IPOs of these businesses due to the Japanese Dotcom fiascoes with 'Mothers' and 'Hercules'. A number of local venture GPs began to raise and invest successfully following the early 2010s, including Globis Capital Partners and Mobile Internet Capital. Nevertheless, actual mentoring of entrepreneurs and moonshot type investments in Japanese Venture was seldom seen.

By the late 2010s, most corporates had established Venturing setups with some establishing third party funds underneath their holdings. Foreign Corporates also remained active in Japanese Venture, notably Salesforce formed a $100mn vehicle, the Salesforce Japan Trailblazer Fund. Amongst Japanese Pharma groups, most had established and mature operations of venture investing in the US, such as Takeda and Taiho Pharmaceuticals, but only by the late 2010s did many establish parallel corporate venture desks in Japan; Taiho formed its domestic fund only in 2019 having been active successfully in US Biotech since 2016. In 2016, almost $2.6bn was invested by Japanese venture GPs into startups there, notably a rise in university vehicles also played an increasing part in the seed stage. Japanese government, through its corporate zombies fund INCJ and its Development Bank DBJ, also began to take an interest in nurturing and expanding the number of sector focussed venture GPs.

Only by 2018, was there rampant activity amongst domestic LPs to set up in-house allocation towards PE. This also led to a number of IR offices opening up as from foreign GPs, including Ardian, EQT, CVC, Apollo, and Partners Group. Despite increasing interest, almost all Japanese Institutional Investors had a 10-20% PE weighting to their own market; with the vast majority of their reups and ongoing legacy GPs focussed on US Growth and Buyouts and Global LargeCaps.

Some early Japanese LP movers struggled to actively manage their portfolio, one in particular include Norinchukin Bank, a large Agricultural and Fisheries Bank, who led an aggressive PE Programme in the mid 2000s so as to act as supplier of debt to underlying deals of its local GPs but eventually much of their PE portfolio was sold to Ardian for $5bn on the secondary market in 2019. A number of foreign insurers with a strong presence in Japan including Canadian Manulife and Prudential, having acquired Gibraltar Life Insurance Company in 2001, were also actively reinvesting premiums from their Japanese balance sheet back into Japanese Private Equity.

During the mid-2010s, Japanese Midmarket GPs also took off on the back of succession-driven transactions amongst Japan's ageing demographic and onerous inheritance tax laws. Most succession transactions were under $9mn in value but almost 650 were recorded between 2012 and 2017.[22] Rise in succession fueled deals was also due to the low but fiercely competitive and auctioned Japanese corporate carevout deals. On the largecap, Bain Capital led consortium took Toshiba's memory unit for $18bn market, a high point in 2017 of foreign GP activity in Japan; KKR's $3.3bn acquisition of Calsonic Kansei was another. Bain had some success in Japan already when its $67mn buyout of the Domino's Pizza Franchise produced a IRR of 156% over seven years.[23]

By 2017, A number of homegrown GPs, a second wave following from the earlier 2000s GP generation, set up shop; including NSSK and, then in 2019, T Capital Partners, a management buyout of Tokio Marine Private Equity. Amongst the large cap foreign GPs, by 2019, only Carlyle had formed a standalone Japan fund, most kept their Japan allocation through their opportunistic global and pan Asian

---

[22] "Destination: Japan", Private Equity International, 8th March 2018.
[23] "Bain Capital leads the charge as Japan's private equity dealmaking picks up", Plus Company Updates, 12th October 2017.

pockets; by 2019, KKR had five investments in its then portfolio, CVC had made four Japanese deals upto then.[24]

---

[24] "Why global firms are marching on Japan", Private Equity International, 9th April 2019.

Korea

Korea

Selected Private Market Funds

1990	1990- TONGYANG No.1 Venture Investment Partnership KRW 7bn
	1996- TONGYANG No.4 Venture Investment Partnership KRW 20bn
2000	1999- Hyundai-Daum internet Fund I KRW 10bn
	1999- KTIC 9 KRW 40bn
	2000- Hanwha Venture Investment Partnership No.1 KRW 10bn
	2000- TONGYANG No.10 Venture Investment Partnership KRW 10bn
	2000- Hyundai Biotech Fund I KRW5bn
	2003- Busan Venture Investment Fund No.2 KRW 11bn
	2004- HVIC IT Fund III
	2004- KTIC CRC 3 KRW 727bn
	2005- Macquarie Korea Opportunities Fund $1.2bn
	2006- KTIC CRC 6 KRW 65bn
	2007- KTIC CRC 8 KRW 120bn
	2007- IDG Korea Fund $100mn
2010	2010- Macquarie Korea Opportunities Fund II $1bn
	2011- Hahn & Company Fund I $750mn
	2011- SB Pan-Asia Fund $84mn
	2011- IMM RoseGold PEF II $657mn
	2013- MBK Partners III $2.7bn
	2015- EastBridge Asian Mid-Market Opportunities Fund II $190mn
	2015- Hahn & Company Fund II $1.2bn
	2016- IMM RoseGold PEF III $1.1bn
	2016- MBK Partners IV $4.1bn
2020	2019- Hahn & Company Fund III $2.7bn
	2020- MBK Partners V $6.5bn

Korean Private Equity Deal Flow is increasingly coming out of corporate carve outs from Chaebols and Industrial Groups. During the mid-2010s, the predominant source of largecap transactions in Korean PE was mostly from exits of international corporates, including MBK Partners buying Homeplus from Tesco, Carlyle taking ADT Korea from Tyco, and MBK buying ING's Korean Life Insurance business. Exit routes for Korean GPs had also evolved over the two decades to 2020, prior to the 2008 GFC almost 75% were sales to strategic investors which had dropped to 50% by 2017.[25] Almost $14bn in PE Exits were achieved in 2018.

---

[25] "The continued rise of South Korean private equity", McKinsey & Company, 17th July 2018.

Following the 1997 Asian Financial Crisis, some foreign GPs chose to remain including Lone Star and Goldman Sachs. Goldman itself became by 2005 the largest shareholder in Korea's fourth largest lender, Hana Bank, providing much needed consolidation in a fragmented Banking market upto then; Goldman also took a 9.7% stake in Kookmin Bank. Lone Star had more difficulty in Korea, especially with its infamous exit of Korea Exchange Bank to HSBC and Hana Financial Group of its controlling 51% stake, originally transacted in 2003, which was repeatedly delayed by the Korean Government leading to an unresolved dispute on price and tax between the latter and Lone Star.[26] Other Foreign players included H&Q who acquired Ssang Yong, a securities unit of the eponymous chaebol, for $30mn in 1998. Newbridge and Carlyle too were active in taking stakes in Korean Banks. Many of these foreign GPs had exited by 2008, the onset of the GFC, understandably as many began to reweight their pan-Asian allocation towards China and India leading to pressures to exit some of their Korean Portfolio. Lately leading upto 2020, some Foreign GPs have re-entered Korea bidding alongside local GPs as well as buying strategic management stakes into local Korean GPs, Jabreen Capital from Oman acquiring a 43% stake in EastBridge Partners in 2019.

Domestic GPs only were given the green light following the 2004 law change by the Korean Regulator on Private Equity Capital Gains Tax and Fund Formation. The regulator also started encouraging local

---

[26] "Lone Star seeks $790 mn out-of-court settlement with Korean govt", Maeil Business News Korea, 25th June 2020.

LPs to back these nascent emerging managers. Such was the early success of this move that by 2006, local GPs raised almost $5bn from local Korean LPs. Leaving some foreign GPs to move from growth, distressed and NPLs, to un-auctioned core Infrastructure plays, reflected in Macquarie's Korea Fund whose first investment in 2006 included a 49% stake into SK E&S, Korea's largest gas distributor. By 2015, the Korean Regulator, the FSC, started to allow funds of funds to form for Korean retail investors to invest into the burgeoning local asset class with a minimum subscription of $4200 for individual investors.

Korean venture also took off by the late 2010s, recording $2.9bn in funding in 2018. Korea Venture Investment Corporation ("KVIC"), a government backed vehicle, had invested $2bn into venture capitalists between 2005 and 2015, anchoring almost 380 VC GPs; uniquely KVIC set its own fund of funds' duration to thirty years with no requirements to pay dividends during its fund duration to the government; rather the purpose is to reinvest all returns from previous realised investments. The Law allowing for company formation and listing requirements became more relaxed on KOSDAQ, encouraging a startup scene to blossom. Healthcare Venture still takes the greater share due to maturing of the biotech ecosystem from early stage to IPO in Korea; generating a 36% average return on exits for investors in Healthcare between 2008 and 2017.[27]

---

[27] "Korean private equity: A beginner's guide", Private Equity International, 19th September 2019.

By 2019, many Korean GPs started to raise significant capital from foreign LPs, including from Japan and rest of Asia displacing US Institutional Investors, who were traditionally able to stomach Korea specific funds and also the Korean Nuclear Conflict Risks. Proven exits with average PE returns across the Korean market averaging 20% IRR since 2005 have boosted the appeal of Korean Private Equity amongst foreign LPs.[28]

By the end of 2019 the largest raise in Korean Private Equity was achieved when Hahn & Co. raised its third fund as well as a separate coinvestment sidecar alongside; uniquely they did this for their 2015 second fund as well. Hahn & Co. gathered $3.2 billion from investors from North America and almost 60% of the sum from Investors from Europe and Asia, taking its overall AUM to $6Bn. Other large GPs active in Korea include IMM with AUM of KRW4.5Tn, MBK with AUM of $16bn, Anchor Equity, and VIG with AUM of KRW2.6Tn. MBK, standing for Michael ByungJu Kim the GP's founder, has been a pioneer since 2004 in establishing the norms for Korean Buyout Investing. Most notably his tough stance in driving a hard price out of ING in July 2013. Most of the leading Korean GPs, have been involved in the gradual restructuring and purchases of non-performing divisions of thinly spread out Korea Chaebols. Hahn bought a controlling stake for $190mn in Woongjin Foods in 2013 from the eponymous group. Vogo too was active in the early 2010s, taking Burger King Franchise from Doosan Group. Much of this

---

[28] "Korean private equity: A beginner's guide", Private Equity International, 19th September 2019.

restructuring was aligned with both the Chaebols, Regulator, and the Korean Banks who wanted to see further Corporate Deleveraging.

Given the nuances of Korea Corporate Governance, a rising trend has occurred of Korean activist investors raising blind pool unlisted vehicles, akin to private equity funds, to buy and then influence into poorly managed and staid conglomerate businesses. One such is KCGI, which raised more than $130mn, investing on the theme of the 'Korean Discount' built in by one of the lowest dividend payout ratios amongst advanced economies and very poor governance. KCGI founder Kang sung-boo is the former CEO of LK Partners who led the firm's investment in Hyundai Cement and Yojin Engineering and is considered a pioneer of Korean shareholder activism. KCGI's most notable influence by 2020 had been into the parent company of Korean Air, Hanjin Kal, initially to mitigate the undervaluation coming from the poor leadership of the Cho family who controlled the group, and following the patriarch's passing in 2019, KCGI began to direct the business. Very savvy and structured model of private equity suited to Korean Corporates; albeit only a handful such activists exist in Korea's closed knit corporate culture.

Many Korean Life Insurers and mid-sized pension funds are still very slow and tedious for their own domestic private equity firms to raise money from; much of the funding from Korean Domestic Investors comes from its large state pension fund, NPS. Increasingly many of the smaller pension and institutional investors, due to regulatory and public scrutiny, rely upon open RFPs from GPs, foreign and domestic.

Many do not have internal risk and managerial selection capabilities providing them with a naive allocation exposure.

Some business groups, such as SK, LG, Lotte, CJ and Kolon, indirectly have corporate VC units outside their holding firms or in the form of overseas affiliates. The Fair Trade Commission in Korea had recommended by the end of 2020 for the conglomerates to own VC units in the form of a wholly owned subsidiary. Allowing corporate VC units to borrow within 200% of their equity capital. When creating a fund, external capital can be brought in upto 40% of the fund size; mirroring similar initiatives in Australia, Japan, and Taiwan. Overseas investments from these Corporate VCs would also be allowed for up to 20% of their total assets.[29]

---

[29] The Investor Korea, 'Korea allows large firms to hold venture capital units', July 30, 2020.

South East Asia

South East Asia

Selected
Private Market
Funds

1990	1988- Vertex Investment I $35mn
	1995- Vertex Investment II $70mn
	1996- Lombard Pacific Partners $400mn
	1996- Vertex Investment III $37mn
	1997- Vertex Technology Fund $95mn
	1999- Navis Asia Fund I $68mn
2000	1999- Vertex Technology Fund II $150mn
	2001- Lombard Thailand Equity Fund $245mn
	2002- Mekong Enterprise Fund $19mn
	2005- Navis Asia Fund IV $315mn
	2005- Gobi Fund I $52mn
	2006- Lombard Asia III $240mn
	2006- Mekong Enterprise Fund II $50mn
	2007- Navis Asia Fund V $1bn
	2008- Vietnam Investments Fund I $100mn
	2010- Northstar Equity Partners II $285mn
2010	2010- Navis Asia Fund VI $1.2Bn
	2011- Northstar Equity Partners III $820mn
	2013- Myanmar Opportunities Fund I $50mn
	2013- Lombard Asia IV $350mn
	2015- Northstar Equity Partners IV $810mn
	2015- Navis Asia Fund VII $1.5Bn
	2015- Falcon House Partners Fund II, L.P. $400mn
	2016- Mekong Enterprise Fund III $112mn
	2016- Jungle Ventures II $100mn
	2017- Vickers Venture Partners V $230mn
	2018- Myanmar Opportunities Fund II $70mn
2020	2019- Jungle Ventures III $240mn

Despite these disparate economies in South East Asia (SE Asia), some developed and others still dirt poor, the region is collated in this book as a single chapter due to the shared impact of private equity and its corporate governance maturity therein since the East Asian Financial Crisis of 1997. Singapore and its global emergence in the three decades from 1990 to 2020 also acts as a lynchpin for the success story of private equity here. Stability and security of investment as well as rising technology usage and middle class growth, has led to a record $23.5Bn in Private Equity and Venture Investments made in 2017 in the region. Asean Economic Community also has been a cohesive carpet knitting the different fabrics of the South East Asian Economic systems together. Notably in 2018 it abolished all tariffs in the bloc giving local businesses a framework and incentive to establish cross border corporate strategies and vertical linkages across SE Asia. Nevertheless, lack of a common economic union with a shared currency, and regulatory and legal arbitrage limits any further integration of Private Equity in SE Asia into the 21st Century.

There are now more than hundred local venture capital firms focused on south-east Asian start-ups, mostly based in Singapore. East Asian corporate investors, such as China's Alibaba and Tencent, Korea's Hanwha and Samsung, have also shown interest in start-ups as both investors and acquirers and have formed regional hubs out of Singapore to invest into South East Asia. Singapore provides institutional legal security and acts as a source of global talent and entrepot to the region. Temasek, its Sovereign Fund, introduced a retail platform called Azalea in 2006 to Singaporean retail investors who would want to share the benefits of private equity access. Hitherto, Azalea issued five bond financed funds with coupon and liquidity provided through the local stock exchange.

Singapore has also encouraged local SE Asia funds in establishing their structure in Singapore as well as providing regulator and government support in anchor capital as well as matching funding; startups which also got too big for their host country have reincorporated in Singapore, most notoriously the move of Grab from Kuala Lumpur to Singapore in 2014. A successive wave of increasingly easy regulatory regimes in Singapore under MAS, allowed for faster fund formation especially in venture which by end of 2018 led to MAS launching a $5bn fund to anchor fund managers moving to Singapore.

Following the 1997 Asian Financial Crisis, many US Venture GPs retreated to Hong Kong and shut up shop in the region; including Baring PE, HarbourVest, Pantheon, and 3i. The growth of Private Equity following the crisis was led mostly by Singapore, whose venture assets rose to $10Bn by 2003, and in small part by Malaysia and Thailand. Indigenous sovereign backing as well as Asian strategics who remained, such as Hitachi, Samsung, and Acer, provided the initial boost to venture funding in SE Asia. Some of these by 2010s formed strategic partnerships with local early stage GPs in particular in Singapore; Hanwha formed an evolving partnership from 2014 onwards with Golden Gate Ventures, initially investing in early stages and by 2019 shifting to mid-stage series B+ investing. By the end of the 2010s, what was known as a 'Series A Gap' in SE Asia was transformed into a more structured process for venture funding from seed to late stage. The marquee venture investments in SE Asia include Grab and Go-Jek, each commanding private valuations above $10bn by end of 2019; and Singapore alone hosting 11 unicorns by 2019.

From 2001 to 2011, Private Equity AUM in SE Asia rose from $11.7bn to $30.1bn.[30] Some local GP players, who in turn raised larger successor funds into the 2010s, scored a number of record-returning

---

[30]"Southeast Asia lures private equity, but dealmaking challenges grow", Hedgeweek, 6th December 2012.

low hanging fruits from their earlier funds raised in the decade following 1997. Mekong's second Vietnamese fund delivered a 4.5x multiple on its $50mn committed capital with a standout return of 50x in ten years on its 2007 $3.5mn investment into Mobile World.[31] Similarly an early success in Indonesia was the 2002 investment made by Farallon Capital Management into PT Bank Central Asia paying $567mn for a 51% stake and raking in more than a $1bn in returned capital on the initial investment by 2009.[32] Despite these successes, local and regional exit markets still remained behind India and China, and with many local listed peers numbering less than 5 in any given sector in SE Asia leading to mis-pricing on IPO of PE backed businesses.

In Malaysia, much of the ecosystem GPs have been supported by its local Institutional Giants, Employees Provident Fund and Ekuinas. Most local GPs have been active following the 2008 GFC in Consumer Goods, Healthcare, Education, and Telco Sectors. Malaysian Venture have been aided by the rising penetration of digital consumption of goods and services by its middle class.

By the mid 2010s, the region's deal market was mostly driven by Singapore, Indonesia and Malaysia, which together made up more than 80% of PE deal value from 2012 to 2016. Institutional Investors also overtook local and regional family offices as the primary LP

[31] "Changing dynamics provide opportunity in South-East Asia", Private Equity International, 11th December 2018.
[32] "Indonesia : Private Equity Stars Aligning for Stable Indonesia", TendersInfo, December 14th 2009.

backers of SE Asia Funds. Some invest in addition to the flagship funds of their GPs, alongside them in separate side cards to raise their overall weighting as well as provide some control on additional investments.

In Thailand, overcrowding across multiple sectors resulted from the dominance of their 'five family' conglomerates across industries; most prominent of the five was CP Group headed by the Chearavanont Family whose ancestral links to China allowed them to operate crossborder, becoming at one point the largest shareholder in Ping An Insurance. The dominance at the larger end of the market, has led to the birth of a number of successful GPs such as Lakeshore Capital in the 2010s, active in the Thai MidMarket taking minority stakes in investment of up to $50mn.

In the Philippines, Navegar gained prominence in partnership with Swedish Alternatives Firm, Brummer & Partners, in marking out its mid market territory. Brummer was behind Navegar, having brought in IFC and other Foreign LPs and providing much needed credibility to an indigenous Filipino PE firm. Much of the largecap deals in the mid-2010s there were carried out by corporates and pan-Asian GPs, including CVC taking SPi Global for $200mn, Capital International buying ABS-CBN, and GIC, the Singaporean Sovereign Fund, becoming increasingly active across the board investing alongside KKR into Metro Pacific Hospital. Like in Thailand, a number of successful Chinese Diaspora Families ran the country's leading conglomerates, including Sy Family behind SM Investments and Tan

Family behind LT Group. The influence of these family corporates limited the initial penetration of PE in the country, and in fact the first major PE deal was carried out only in 2008 by Ashmore, investing into a state mining firm, Petron.

In Vietnam, a number of foreign GPs have been active there; Techcombank ahead of its listing in Ho Chi Minh sold a $370mn stake in 2018 to Warburg Pincus. Warburg itself has had a successful record in Vietnam making almost a 10x multiple on its retail investment into Vincom Retail, a shopping mall owner operator. Warburg prior to the pandemic closed its second regional fund, Warburg Pincus China-Southeast Asia II, at $4.25bn having completed by 2019 five investments in Vietnam, three in Singapore, and two in Indonesia from all its global and local vehicles. This follows CVC allocated more than half its fifth asian fund to South East Asia as well as Morgan Stanley raising an oversubscribed country specific Thai fund at $440mn in 2018.

Vietnam has stood out, at least compared to Thailand and Malaysia, in booming from the gains in AUM in Asian Private Equity in the 2010s. A number of pan asian funds situated out of Hong Kong and Singapore have been active in Vietnamese PE, including Blackstone, Carlyle, and KKR. TPG has been active in brewing in the region, having acquired 50% stake in Myanmar Distillery in 2015 and exited at 3x its stake in ThaiBev in 2017. Most PE opportunities in Vietnam in the two decades upto 2020 stemmed from the privatisation of state owned enterprises focussing mostly on consumer and industrials; the next PE-led drive going into the 2020s will be through SE Asian Corporates, both privately held and public, divesting non-core parts.

Many of the regions' GPs have also brought in outsiders and foreigners into boards and businesses to instill transparency and best practices; notably Creador in Malaysia and Mekong Capital in Vietnam have tapped into their respective diaspora networks for executives based in the US and Europe. Some GPs have been formed purely for successful entrepreneurs to reinvest back into their home countries, such was the instance behind Myanmar-focussed Ascent Capital Partners, registered in Singapore, and anchored by Moe Kyaw, founder of Myanmar Distillery, and Tony Chew, who had been active in Myanmar for two decades.

The opening of Myanmar in the latter half of 2010s shares some of the same features with the success story of Vietnamese Private Equity, which had succeeded against the backdrop of state dirigisme, autocratic rule, and arbitrary rule of law. Most Myanmar funds would be structured out of Singapore, including Mandalay Capital, Golden Rock Capital, and PMM Partners. Investment Restrictions included exit routes, as the local stock exchange only allowed fully Myanmar owned businesses to list. This however did not stop larger pan-Asian groups to make their first forays there, including TPG who invested over $200mn in 2014 in Apollo Towers, a telco provider, and Distillery Company. But even by the 2020s, much of the private equity interest from Foreign LPs was limited to Development

Financial Institutions who provided the anchor capital through an Impact and ESG Lense.

Northstar has acted as a catalyst for Private Equity in Indonesia in particular. The GP's portfolio includes ride-hailing platform Gojek, minimarket chain Indomarket and real estate brokerage APAC Realty. Gojek itself was supported by international strategic and private equity players, including a KKR investment in 2016 amounting to $550mn. Traditionally, following 1997, much of PE interest from foreign players into Indonesia was energy and commodity focussed; lately in the five years leading up to 2020, consumer sectors have taken the lion's share. Warburg Pincus' first investment into Indonesia in 2014 replicated its success in China and elsewhere by investing into a JV with a local operator to develop retail malls.

By 2020, Indonesia overtook Malaysia as the second largest venture market in SE Asia, with East Ventures most active and crossborder funds, even from outside of Asia such as Finch Capital from Netherlands having a deeper presence there. A number of existing family houses in Jakarta had also been active in venture during the decade upto 2020, including Salim Family, Astra Ventura of PT Astra, and Sinar Mas Ventura of Widjaja Family. The Salim family had formed a number of JV with VC GPs, including GREE Ventures from Japan, and through their Indofood group were actively seeking FoodTech, Ecommerce, and Delivery startups.

In Singapore the city-state Reits, with a heavy weighting of commercial and retail properties, were considered safe havens for retail investors in the two decades of the 21st Century. Demand for commercial and retail property has been consistently due to Singapore's tourism sector, which annually attracts about three times its population, providing Reit dividend yields above 5 per cent for the decade leading up to 2020. Listed Reits made up more than a tenth of Singapore's stocks by market value at its height in the 2010s. Facing the symptoms of the Dutch Disease, much of the investments from Singaporean LPs were made outside of its borders due to its own overpriced market across property, private equity, and venture capital.

Following the onset of the 2020 Pandemic, although fundraising has slumped to a record low, SE Asia GPs are sitting on almost $9bn in dry powder.[33] Some of these are also GPs, who closed their next generation funds in 2018 and 2019. In addition as Chinese Strategics have been blacklisted from further investments in India, Europe, Australia, and the US, many of them are seeking to consolidate their SE Asia Portfolio further with addons and new sectoral investments. Sectors adversely affected post-pandemic would mirror those elsewhere globally, retail and travel startups would retreat whereas biotech and software valuations may keep up.

---

[33] "Coronavirus no damper for Southeast Asian private equity firms flush with US$8.7 billion in unspent cash", South China Morning Post, August 26th 2020.

Many of these Chinese strategics going in alone into the 2020s, having started by pairing up with local families or pan Asian GPs, such as Tencents first Filipino deal in 2018 which was alongside KKR into Voyager Innovations. By 2019, some of larger VC Funds from China started to open offices in Singapore, including Qiming Venture Partners and GGC Capital intending to replicate their successful early mover strategies from China into local markets in SE Asia; in particular Qiming backed an Indonesian social ecommerce startup similar to Pinduoduo called Mucho.

India

India

Selected Private Market Funds

1990

1995- GVCF (Gujarat IT Fund) INR600mn

2000

1999-ChrysCapital I $64mn
2000-IVTS I(Ascent) INR 1.1Bn
2001- ICICI Eco-net Internet $20mn

2004-ChrysCapital III $258mn
2006- Matrix Partners India I $150mn
2006- ChrysCapital IV $550mn
2007- ChrysCapital V $1.2bn
2008- Lighthouse India 2020 Fund I $100mn
2008- Kotak India Growth Fund II $440mn

2010

2010-Ascent India Fund III $350mn

2011- Matrix Partners India II $300mn
2012-ChrysCapital VI $510mn
2013- Inventus Capital Partners Fund II $106mn
2013- Golden Gujarat Growth Fund INR 10Bn
2015- Lighthouse India 2020 Fund II $138mn

2017- ChrysCapital VII $600mn
2018- Matrix Partners India III $321mn
2019- Lighthouse India 2020 Fund III $230mn
2019- ChrysCapital VIII $864mn

2020

2019- Kotak Special Situations Fund $1B

The literal dangers of Indian private equity are the high transaction costs of doing business, not just bribery and licencing requirements in most sectors, but the basic infrastructure required for the efficient market flow of labour and goods. Too often half of the day within any major Indian city is spent in bottleneck traffic, as the author himself can testify; aggravated by the poor quality and layout of roads and traffic junctions. These basic deficiencies increase search and due diligence costs for private equity investors; especially those who are managing foreign capital that demands a high threshold for due diligence and portfolio rigour. Many criticize the Chinese for white elephant projects, but the role of the state is to create overexpansion of public goods, including infrastructure, at the risk of crowding out private financing and not knowing which projects would be utilized to near full demand consumption. In the opinion of the Author, for the PE industry to further mature and develop the Indian government, with its scarce resources, should prioritize air routes and better airports for tier I and II cities and modern urban auto and public transport infrastructure for its five most prosperous and largest metropolises: Delhi, Mumbai, Bangalore, Chennai, and Hyderabad. Successful PE investment by the late 2010s in India have been part of the commercial solutions to these bottlenecks. India's logistics market, valued at $160bn, attracted significant foreign VC funding by 2019 including into 'Blackbuck', $150mn from Wellington, Sequoia, and IFC; 'Delhivery', a supply chain startup, taking $670mn from SoftBank and Tiger Global; and 'Rivigo', providing truck drivers, raising $215mn from SAIF Partners and Warburg Pincus.

The height of Indian Private Equity in 2017 resulted in almost $24bn invested through 591 deals. Almost 75% of the activity was from foreign GPs leading to some notable deals including Softbank buying 24% of Flipkart, GIC's $1.4bn investment into DLF Cyber City; Bain Capital taking 10% in Axis Bank. Indian e-commerce was by far the most active sector, taking $6bn in PE investments in 2017. Much of this investment interest and success was built on some large exits carried out in the mid-2010s, including Bain Capital's $640mn exit from Hero MotoCorp and ChrysCapital's 23x return from its $160mn exit from Intas Pharma reputed to be the most successful exit in Indian PE.[34] Some of the other notable exits also shared a Foreign GP-to-GP exit route, including TPG selling 20% stake in Shriram City Union Finance to Apax in 2015 and New Silk Route selling

---

[34] "Record 95 exits in 2014 buoy India private equity play", The Times of India, 25th December 2014.

Destimoney Enterprises, a Financial Service Provider, to Carlyle for almost 9x multiple in 2015.

Despite these successful exits, GP strategy entry pricing on target companies remained an issue for many foreign LPs studying Indian Growth Strategies in the mid-2010s; much of it was skewed by the higher valuations placed on 7000 listed public companies in India compared to its global counterparts. Often domestic midmarket GPs would be buying into 9-12x multiple on earnings compared to 8x seen in South East Asia and lower elsewhere in Asia.[35]

In the early 2000s, notably investments by largecap foreign GPs resulted in some low hanging exits. A number of $1bn deals occurred including into Bharti Infratel by Goldmanc Sachs, Temasek, and Macquarie, and Idea Cellular by TA Associates, Citigroup, GLG Partners, and Sequoia. Warburg Pincus made almost $1.1bn on its 18% stake from a $300mn investments carried out between 1999 and 2001 into Bharti Televentures, renamed Bharti Airtel. Most indigenous GPs in the 200s were considerably smaller and part of existing financial groups, these included UTI Venture, ICICI Venture, and ChrysCaptial. Number of PE deals peaked at 435, total value of $14bn, in 2007 from 83 deals carried out in 2004 at $1.7bn.[36]

Further restrictions in the 2000s to foreign GP activity were the lending restrictions on control deals, leading to foreign GPs often

---

[35] "Private equity in India: Struggling with multiples" Private Equity International, 23rd October 2015.
[36] "After the crash", Private Equity International Asia, October 2008.

placing almost 70-90% of the purchase price from their own equity. Perhaps knowing the cash rich transaction values underpinning foreign GP-led transactions, many Indian promoter target businesses in India in the early 2000s favoured the involvement of foreign GPs, or at second best their own Industrial Groups such as Reliance or Tata, over their own domestic GPs; leading to some local GPs investing into publicly listed companies, PIPE; these PIPE deals amounted to almost $4.4bn in 2007. It reflected also the lack of cyclical discipline and focus of the first generation of indigenous domestic GPs. PIPE deals were all the more surprising as under Insider Trading Regulations of 1992, listed Indian businesses were unable to provide complete due diligence access to potential investors in their stock. Some GPs affected by these PIPE deals were unable to return capital at their fund's term end, one notorious example included Avigo Capital whose second fund from 2005 kept its stake, with a personal investment from the GP founders too, in a target investee called Tecpro. Avigo Capital was only able to return 30% of its invested capital from the second fund and its management for further exits from the second fund was subsequently taken over in an acrimonious battle by one of its foreign LPs, Siguler Guff.

By the late 2010s, a number of spinoff GPs had been created from Sequoia, Matrix, and from domestic Corporate Venturing including from Tata; A91 Partners coming out of Sequoia, Epiq Capital from Matrix, Pravega Ventures from SAIF Partners, SeaLink Capital from KKR. In the instance of Tata, similar to other large trading corporations across Asia who had set up third party vehicles underneath them, the management team were initially allocated paltry carry share amounting to only 40% for deals done over their first fund. This was aided by 2012 regulatory reforms streamlining the registration and regulation of AIFs; building on the earlier LLP reforms under the Limited Liability Partnership Act 2008.

Due to the rising number of active domestic and foreign GPs, a number of GPs invested outside of the traditional sectors of IT, Healthcare, and Financial Services. Baring PE took stakes in 2010 alongside Matrix Partners into a Gold Financing Business, Muthoot Finance. KKR started NBFCs to provide financing. In Venture, a number of US inspired copycat investments, tweaked to India, succeeded in the early 2010s, including Ola, FlipKart, and Paytm. The dominant sectors driving Indian venture included ConsumerTech, Software, FinTech, and B2B Commerce. The notable rise in Indian venture activity by the mid 2015s was also led by foreign GPs, including Sequoia, SAIF Partners, Tiger Global, and Accel Partners. Nevertheless coming upto 2020, Indian Venture still held the promise than actual gains of at least 10x expected, commensurate to the risks in currency and growth presented in India, in certain deals from early stage to late stage investing. Much of the marquee investments in India's start startup success was also skewed by the involvement of Softbank and its vision fund; driving up founder expectations and valuations and leading eventually to mismatched expectations for exits.

Global Secondaries GP also started to take an interest by the late-2010s, in particular into GPs from the first generation of emerging domestic managers unable to raise a second or third fund and from local teams investing for foreign GPs looking for a management spinout. Many first generation Indian GPs, coming to India with US experience, failed to realise the leveraged buyout space in the US was not akin to the minority growth investing suited to India. Increasing number of unsophisticated GPs from the first generation have led to a situation akin to Gresham's Law: the bad sort driving out the good. The actual Gresham Law was prevalent even in Medieval India, when under the Delhi Sultanate in the reign of Muhammad bin Tughluq (1324-51) cheaper coins drove out the silver supply of coins which were hoarded by merchants and tradesman.[37]

Private Equity is hindered in India by its cumbersome labour rules which create incentives for companies either to stay small, to subcontract employment to brokers, and to invest in capital equipment rather than a larger labour intensive workforce. The Industrial Employment Act 1946, for instance, requires any establishment with more than a hundred employees to secure government approval if it wishes to fire anyone, or even to reassign internally.

The 2020 Pandemic has affected India adversely, more so than other Asian PE Markets, on valuations and cash hoarding as well as on deal flow. Amending the Foreign Exchange Management Rules in 2020

---

[37] India in the Persianate Age (1000-1765), Eaton, 2019. Pg 71.

have also affected Chinese inbound PE Investments by restricting further funding from new investors from countries India shares a border with.   Having been established in 2018, the National Investment and Infrastructure Fund carried on its support for funding anchor closes to indigenous GPs during the 2020 Pandemic, and even attracted the $100mn from the Asian Development Bank into its Fund of Funds.[38] In addition Domestic LPs, including Insurers and local Family Offices, became a larger source of fundraising for domestic GPs.

---

[38] "ADB Invests $ 100 Million in NIIF to Support India's Private Equity Industry", ENP Newswire, 31st March 2020.

Australia

Australia

1990

Selected
Private Market
Funds

1996- Quadrant Capital Fund No. 1 AUD50mn
1998- Archer Capital Fund I AUD104mn
1998- Pacific Equity Partners Fund I AUD92mn
1998- Quadrant Capital Fund No. 2 AUD75mn

2000

2001- Quadrant Capital Fund No. 3 AUD125mn
2002- Helmsman Capital Fund AUD41mn
2004- Pacific Equity Partners Fund II AUD316mn
2005- Next Capital I AUD265mn
2005- Quadrant Private Equity No. 1 AUD265mn
2007- Archer Capital Fund IV AUD1.36bn
2007- Macquarie Infrastructure Partners $4bn
2007- Quadrant Private Equity No. 2 AUD500mn
2008- Pacific Equity Partners Fund IV AUD4bn
2009- Next Capital II AUD285mn
2010- Quadrant Private Equity No. 3 AUD 750mn

2010

2011- Archer Capital Fund V AUD1.1bn

2014- Quadrant Private Equity No. 4 AUD850mn
2015- Pacific Equity Partners Fund V AUD2.1bn
2016- Quadrant Private Equity No. 5 AUD980mn
2016- OneVentures Healthcare Fund III AUD170mn
2017- Quadrant Private Equity No. 6 AUD1.15bn
2018- Adamantem Capital Fund I AUD600mn
2018- BGH Capital Fund I AUD2.6bn
2020- 1V Venture Credit Fund AUD80mn
2020- Blackbird Ventures Fund III AUD500mn

2020
2020- Pacific Equity Partners Fund VI AUD2.5bn

A number of factors led to Australian Private Equity and Venture taking off before much of Asia had started. Incorporation in 1992 of Pooled Development Corporations into Australian Tax Law allowed for more flexibility to encourage fund development in the early 1990s, especially in Forestry, Agriculture, and early stage Venture.[39] But the biggest boost was the introduction of compulsory superannuation savings in the early 1990s, some of these super funds in turn invested into the nascent emerging and indigenous private equity managers soaring their commitments from $500mn in 1997 to $7bn by 2004.[40]

---

[39] Research Handbook on Hedge Funds, Private Equity and Alternative Investments, Erskine, 2012, pgs. 406-441.

[40] "Super dollars translate into super deals", Australian Financial Review, September 22nd 2005.

However, Superannuation funds have historically shied away from domestic venture capital, with the first significant backing in the market made by First State Super and HostPlus both backed a $200mn fund established by Blackbird Ventures in 2014; till this much of the ecosystem city based state venture funds sustained by local family offices and corporates, some of the former ranking as the richest in Australia such as the Packer and Pratt Families. 2015 marked a notable high for Australian Venture Capital, as a number of GPs in addition to Blackbird, notably Brandon Capital and Square Peg Capital, raised significant fund sizes amounting to almost $700mn in aggregate in 2015.

In recent years, some startups which have transformed into full fledged businesses have had their founders reinvesting back into the Australian venture scene; most prominent of them is Grok Ventures, the single family office of tech billionaire Mike Cannon-Brookes founder of Atlassian, which having been backed by Accel Partners in 2010 went on to IPO on the NASDAQ in 2015 at $4.4Bn. Some of the reluctance to provide institutional super backing for Venture has also stemmed from the performance for Australian VC which has historically been even worse than in the US, with only a quarter of funds generating positive returns for their investors.[41] By 2020, Australia's leading venture GP, Blackbird managed almost AUD 1.24

---

[41] "Australian venture capital level is 'woeful'; Private equity", Australian Financial Review, March 4th 2017.

billion in committed capital achieving an net internal rate of return of 46.7%.[42]

Furthermore, Australian Venture has seen the rise of corporate strategics participating and leading at an earlier stage into startup funding rounds. Telstra Ventures active since 2011 and Seven West Media both jointly backed HealthEngine, an online health directory, for $5.2Mn apiece in 2013. By 2018, Telstra rolled its existing investments into a fund structure which included a secondary and primary commitment from HarbourVest. Other property groups such as Salta and Grollo formed Property-tech vehicles to support their businesses as well as gaining international venture partnerships.

Initially most Private Equity GPs were Sydney based due to lifestyle and consulting and banking backgrounds. In the last decade leading up to 2020, a number of new GPs have been formed catering to their local lower midmarket businesses across South and West Australia as well as smaller fund formations in second tier cities such as Liverpool, Gold Coast, and Newcastle.

Secondary factors which also led to the independent birth of alternative investing in Australia was the institutional stability provided by the rule of law, sound macroeconomic management which led to low inflation and interest rates, and an open economy with a floating exchange rate in the form of the AUD. By 2010, almost

---

[42] "Cannon-Brookes joins Blackbird flock as chair; Venture capital", Sydney Morning Herald, August 5th 2020.

AUD24.5bn was managed in Private Equity, equally more in Infrastructure and the REIT sector AUD60obn and AUD78.2bn respectively. Amongst the most popular investment sectors for PE in 2010 were Retail and Consumer at 30% of funds invested, Energy at 24%, and Business Services and Industrials at 15%.[43]

Compared with its Asian Counterparts, Australian Private Equity was relatively more active in the 2004-2008 Global M&A boom period prior to the GFC; in particular on the large cap segment which included failed bids for Qantas at $8.3bn and Coles Myer at $14.4bn. [44] So much so was it a favoured destination for Global PE, Australia accounted for more than a third of total Asia-Pacific PE deals in 2006. Equally international GPs, such as KKR and Carlyle, were active in the Australian market and which attracted increasing public scrutiny for the first time of the role of private equity in the Australian economy. In 2007, the Takeovers Panel and Reserve Bank of Australia established guidelines regulating conflict of interest and market impact of private equity bids.[45] Many Australian Boards also have a built in suspicion of foreign private equity, stemming in particular from non-exec board members, who are prone to media leakage.[46] By 2020 during the pandemic, the regulatory screening thresholds from foreign buyers for all sectors and foreign investor

---

[43] Research Handbook on Hedge Funds, Private Equity and Alternative Investments, Erskine, 2012,, pg 424.
[44] The Oxford Handbook of Private Equity, Cumming. Pg. 673.
[45] Research Handbook on Hedge Funds, Private Equity and Alternative Investments, Erskine, 2012, pg. 424.
[46] "U.S. Private Equity Firms Find a Chilly Reception in Australia", The New York Times, March 24th 2015.

types were reduced to AUD 0 and the Foreign Investment Review Board assessment process extended from 30 days to six months.

The Government funded IIF Program established in 1997 encouraged the growth of Australia Venture by providing matching funding to GPs own capital raises.[47] Government funding has lately also become sector specific, with Medical venture capital fund Brandon Capital selected to manage the lion's share of the government's $500 million Biomedical Translation Fund, which is aiming to bridge the funding gap between early stage pharmaceutical and medtech startups and commercialisation. Australia has a long history of being strong in scientific research in particular within engineering and medicine, but weak in the commercialisation of it, resulting in the past the premature exits of homegrown players such as Spinifex, which was acquired by Novatis for more than $200mn, and Fibrotech which shifted its business outside of Australia.

Private capital assets in Australia reached a record $68bn in 2019, with almost $25bn in Private Equity AUM, and with almost $13bn available in dry powder by 2020 during the Pandemic to invest. In 2019, major PE deals included Silver Lake 's $1.3bn acquisition of ticketing business TEG in October 2019 and KKR's $1.1bn investment into Colonial First State. Trade buyers have been the main beneficiaries on exit over public IPOs. Strategics accounted for more than 70 percent of exits in Australian PE in 2019, compared with just

---

[47] 'Venture's economic impact in Australia', Cumming and Johan. The Journal of Technology Transfer. February 2016, 41(1):25-59.

over half in 2017. Overall IRR for Australian PE since 2009 has been around 20%.[48]

Even during the mid 2010s Private Equity was suffering from a bad reputation in the Australian Press. Dick Smith which had been sold by Woolworths to Anchorage Capital Partners for $94mn in 2012 was quickly listed by the buyer for $520mn but subsequently collapsed by 2015 earning the chagrin of public retail investors. AVCAL, the Private Equity Association for Australia, lobbied and also released research into the public domain highlighting the benefits of Private Equity to the Australian Economy, in a 2013 report it claimed almost half a million jobs were supported by the industry with AUD58bn support to the Australian GDP.[49]

Going forward, both foreign and new domestic players, such as BGH Capital, will continue to dominate the large cap segment in Australia. Foreign GPs have struggled the past decade and a half competing in the $1-3bn segment of the Australian Market, between 2004 and 2015 Bain, Blackstone, Carlyle, KKR, and TPG completed 17 deals in Australia compared to the 337 buyout transaction in the same period. Most notably, Bain Capital bought Virgin Australia from Bankruptcy Protection, having been adversely impacted by the 2020 Pandemic.

---

[48] "Australian private equity in five charts", Private Equity International, 1st August 2019.
[49] "Private equity investment in Australia supports half a million jobs", Hedgeweek, March 8th 2013.

Strategics and Australian Supers will increasingly be prominent as well in auctioned and proprietary deal flow. The supers are also in a merger wave where many of them are consolidating to reduce costs and leverage their size for access and pricing from both managers and sellers; First State Super and VicSuper merged in 2020 to create a AUD 128bn superfund, while MTAA Super and Tasplan are in talks to create a AUD24bn tie-up. In 2019, QSuper and Sunsuper began initial discussions to create a AUD188bn entity, and Hostplus completed a merger with the $600mn Club Super.

Strategics were more prominent in the decade leading up to 2020 attaching themselves to existing Australian GPs and buying from them; Pacific Equity Partners sold Allied Pinnacle for $950mn to Nisshin Foods from Japan; Li Ka Shing's Cheung Kong Infrastructure Holdings already a majority holder of ETSA Utilities, South Australia's electricity distributor was however blocked to take over AusGrid, the national network. Further Chinese interests were torpedoed including Mengniu Dairy's offer to buy Lion Dairy despite having brough Bellamy's in 2019 and another rejection followed by a Chinese consortium to take over cattle ranches, S Kidman & Co. Following the 2020 Pandemic it is likely that Australian businesses will be protected from further Asian attempts to buy them, in particular from Strategic Buyers, and European and US Private Equity Players would have an open door into Australian private markets into the mid 2020s. Encouraging a tighter grip of the GP-LP relationships for those seeking access to Australia.

Conclusion

Rather than providing a summary of what's hitherto been written, the focus of this concluding note would be to look ahead to the future and understand the dynamics of private equity within Asia into the 2020s and 2030s.

National Startup Sovereign Development Funds are seizing the initiative to anchor first time managers as well as provide anchor support to the continued development of their existing GPs. Many of these development funds in Asia are well financed and also acting as credible sources of public money and rubber stamps for other Foreign and domestic LPs to ride the coat-tails of. Additionally, sector specific and buyout strategies are gaining traction in Asian markets, at the risk of creating GP hubris of these nascent focus areas which was all too common in the initial growth GPs of the first generation of Asian managers, as highlighted in the chapters hitherto.

Indigenous Asian GPs are overtaking global large cap funds in dominating the mid- to large-cap and corporate carveout markets in their own countries. Often encouraged by corporate insiders and state apparatus to take these positions. What these domestic GPs may lack in risk and governance mechanisms, compared to their international counterparts, they make up in deal access and pricing. Nevertheless, to attract foreign LPs many would need to incorporate the practices and transparency required by their foreign GP counterparts.

Increasing regulatory and capital restrictions would allow for venture backed market leaders being formed nationally within the borders of Asian economies. Global GPs and strategic corporates from ride hailing to food delivery would struggle to access these regulated markets as majority owners. From India to Australia, governments would have an impulse in the 2020s to protect and nurture the shareholder base of national data-driven champions. Nevertheless, the successful return produced in Asia in the two decades between 1997 and late 2010s was mostly by pan Asian GPs identifying at an early stage national champions who were able to seize the position of winner takes all market. Increasingly following the 2020s, many of the traditional pan-Asian buyout GPs are placing money into locally backed rising champions, such as KKR's 2.3% stake made in 2020 into Reliance's Jio platforms coming from both its Buyout pocked and global tech fund.

Increasing use of SPACs in the US by 2020 to take private companies public and bypassing the IPO process has led to a number of GPs and

Entrepreneurs filing for these types of blank cheque vehicles, often with similar structure to PE in compensation and term. SPACs usually allow the sponsor around two to three years to identify the targets as well as giving the sponsor upto 20% of the target company following a merger being agreed with the SPAC. In Asia, for regulatory and novelty reasons, SPACs had not taken off but a number of deals were prominent by mid-2020; including Vistas Media Capital raising a $100mn SPAC in Singapore focussing on media and entertainment and Hong Kong based D8 Holdings raising $300mn on the NYSE for Consumer Brands. These structures rely upon sponsor counterparties to have a deep track record and expertise in negotiating and identifying their targets as well as public market appetite to back these sponsors; nevertheless SPACs lack the formality and depth which a GP-LP Structure provides to nurture and enhance the businesses with portfolio and size diversification as well as flexibility to be acyclical.

The decade prior to 2020, a number of GPs across Asia and elsewhere tended to use subscription credit lines to fund their capital calls providing themselves flexibility to deal make as well as giving their LPs more room on providing the eventual capital call. As the Pandemic hit in 2020, a number of GPs closed these lines fearing LP liquidity would restrict actual capital calls as well as relying on a certain number of creditworthy LPs in their funds to make the capital calls happen against the closing credit lines. In Asia in particular where a large variation of LP quality exists in certain GP Funds, this liquidity crisis amongst LPs can lead to a number of fund runs as well as potential for escalating Banking Crisis in the event the repayments on subscription lines are not met against the illiquid fund portfolio; a point raised in an interview by the Australian Super Fund.[50]

Overall, the Asian Private Equity scene has matured and formed a key component to the Asian success story; lifting hundreds of millions out of poverty from the 1990s to 2020 and providing employment and purpose to countless lives. US and European Foreign GPs and LPs have complemented its maturity and provided best practices and GP human resources for individual countries to develop their own indigenous set of GPs. Looking into 2020 and beyond, it is hard to doubt that its continued rising involvement as a proportion of Asian GDP would continue. The hiccups may occur where the basics are not practiced, in mis-reporting and valuing underlying targets, fraud, and lack of transparency and good GP governance. Only through continued due diligence, monitoring, and providing sound advice to Asian public policy, can LPs assuage these hiccups and contribute to the re-rise of Asia as the centre of economic activity and trade in the mid-21st century.

---

[50] "Future Fund: Sub lines make it crucial to assess LP creditworthiness", Private Equity International, 17th September 2020.

References

In addition to thanking the valuable input and shared articles provided by reviewers, the fund sizes and fund names with vintage years at the beginning of each of the country chapters is the author's own works and reflects publicly disclosed information by the respective GPs. Further data on domestic country GPs in Asia are available at the following respective regulatory and association websites:

Australia

https://www.avcal.com.au/

https://asic.gov.au/

India

https://ivca.in/

https://www.sebi.gov.in/

Korea

http://www.kvca.or.kr/en/

http://meng.fsc.go.kr/

China

http://www.cvca.org.cn/aboutcvca/profile.asp

http://www.cbrc.gov.cn/showyjhjjindex.do

Japan

http://www.japanpea.jp/english/about/index.html

https://jvca.jp/en/members/vc-members

https://www.fsa.go.jp/en/

Singapore (South East Asia)

https://www.svca.org.sg/

https://www.mas.gov.sg/

The remaining references are alphabetically listed below by titles:

1	"ADB Invests $ 100 Million in NIIF to Support India's Private Equity Industry", ENP Newswire, 31st March 2020.

2	"After the crash", Private Equity International Asia, October 2008.

3	"Australian private equity in five charts", Private Equity International, 1st August 2019.

4	"Australian venture capital level is 'woeful'; Private equity", Australian Financial Review, March 4th 2017.

5	"Bain Capital leads the charge as Japan's private equity dealmaking picks up", Plus Company Updates, 12th October 2017.

6	"Big in Japan", PEI Asia, March 2007.

7	"Can KKR expand from buyouts to backing young tech in Asia?", Financial Times, 16th September 2020.

8	"Cannon-Brookes joins Blackbird flock as chair; Venture capital", Sydney Morning Herald, August 5th 2020.

9	"Changing dynamics provide opportunity in South-East Asia", Private Equity International, 11th December 2018.

10	"China private equity funds suffer wave of closures", Financial Times, 5th August 2018.

11	"China Private Equity hit by share downturn", Financial Times, 15th March 2019.

12	"Coronavirus no damper for Southeast Asian private equity firms flush with US$8.7 billion in unspent cash", South China Morning Post, August 26th 2020.

13   "Destination: Japan", Private Equity International, 8th March 2018.

14   "Foreign private equity funds aim to act local in China", Global Capital Asiamoney, September 2010.

15   "Future Fund: Sub lines make it crucial to assess LP creditworthiness", Private Equity International, 17th September 2020.

16   "Has Asia's safe haven been oversold?", Euromoney, September 2002.

17   "In search of alpha: Updating the playbook for private equity in China", McKinsey & Company, 27th August 2020.

18   "Indonesia : Private Equity Stars Aligning for Stable Indonesia", TendersInfo, December 14th 2009.

19   "Insurers gain a craving for China private equity", AsianInvestor, 30th June 2019.

20   "Inventis: In search of China's 'largest' PE firm", Private Equity International, 8th October 2018.

21   "Is Asian private equity still an attractive play?" Business Times Singapore, 29th May 2019.

22   "Korean private equity: A beginner's guide", Private Equity International, 19th September 2019.

23   "Lone Star seeks $790 mn out-of-court settlement with Korean govt", Maeil Business News Korea, 25th June 2020.

24   "Private Equity in China: Which Way Out?", New York Times, 10th January 2013.

25   "Private equity in India: Struggling with multiples" Private Equity International, 23rd October 2015.

26 "Private equity investment in Australia supports half a million jobs", Hedgeweek, March 8th 2013.

27 "Private Equity, All Aboard?", Newstex Web Blogs, 19th October 2010.

28 "Record 95 exits in 2014 buoy India private equity play", The Times of India, 25th December 2014.

29 "Southeast Asia lures private equity, but dealmaking challenges grow", Hedgeweek, 6th December 2012.

30 "Super dollars translate into super deals", Australian Financial Review, September 22nd 2005.

31 "The continued rise of South Korean private equity", McKinsey & Company, 17th July 2018.

32 "The Long Goodbye", Finance Asia, 26th September 2016.

33 "The Private Equity Limited Partnership in China: A Critical Evaluation of Active Limited Partners.", Lin, Journal of Corporate Law Studies, Vol. 13, No. 1, pp. 185-217, April 2013.

34 "Turnaround of the Year: Shinsei Bank", Buyouts Insider, 14th February 2015.

35 "U.S. Private Equity Firms Find a Chilly Reception in Australia", The New York Times, March 24th 2015.

36 "Venture's economic impact in Australia", Cumming and Johan. The Journal of Technology Transfer. February 2016, 41(1):25-59.

37 "What lies ahead for China private equity", Private Equity International, 19th October 2017.

38 "Why global firms are marching on Japan", Private Equity International, 9th April 2019.

39   China as an Innovation Nation, Zhou, Lazonick, and Sun, 2019.

40   India in the Persianate Age (1000-1765), Eaton, 2019. Pg 71.

41   Innovation in China: Challenging the Global Science and Technology System, Appelbaum, Cao, Han, Parker, and Simon, John Wiley & Sons, 2018.

42   M&A Finance, Sasayama and Muraoka, 2006, pg. 38.

43   Research Handbook on Hedge Funds, Private Equity and Alternative Investments, Erskine, 2012, pg. 424.

44   The Investor Korea, 'Korea allows large firms to hold venture capital units', July 30, 2020.

45   The Oxford Handbook of Private Equity, Cumming. Pg. 673.

[Page left intentionally blank]

[Page left intentionally blank]

[Page left intentionally blank]

Other published works by the Author:

Power and Capital: A Global History of Private Capital (2019)

An Essay on the Tiles of Cádiz (2018)

U.S., Japanese, and German Forex Interventions, 1973-2004 (2017)

[Page left intentionally blank]

[Page left intentionally blank]

[Page left intentionally blank]

[Page left intentionally blank]

[Page left intentionally blank]

Printed in Great Britain
by Amazon

57830266R00061